On Block

Alan Rubin

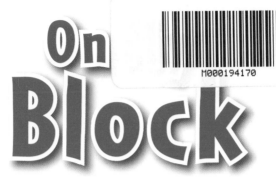

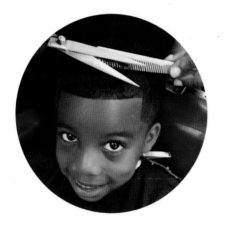

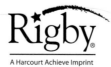

A Harcourt Achieve Imprint

www.Rigby.com
1-800-531-5015

You can get apples.

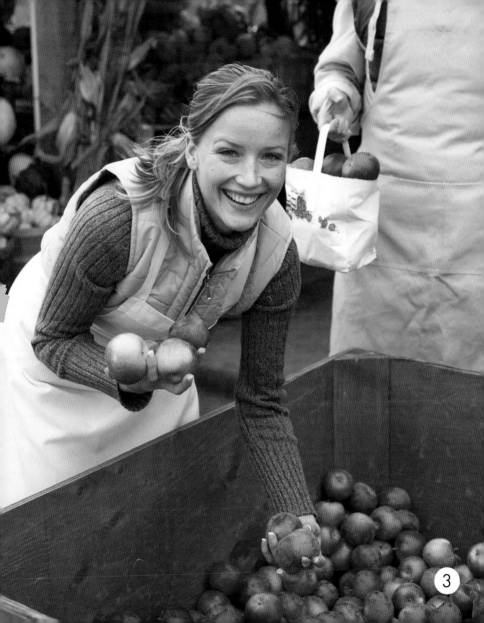

3

You can get bread.

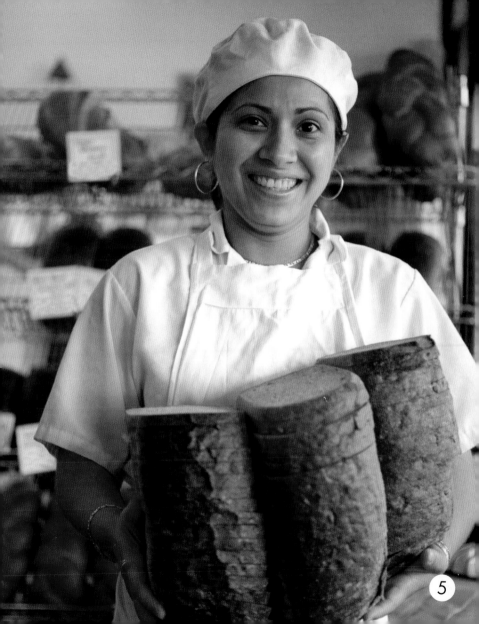

You can get hats.

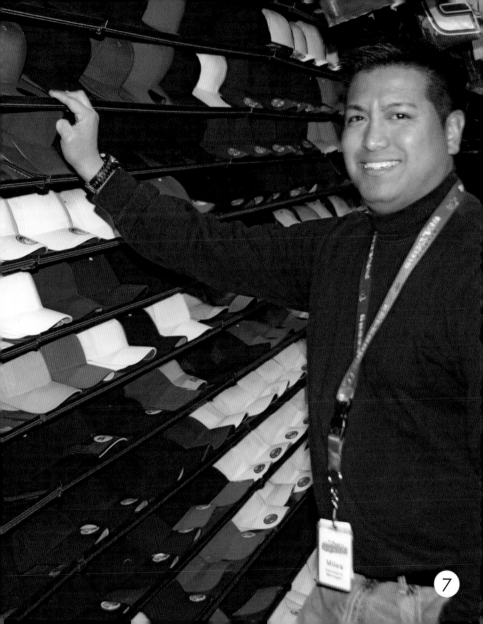

You can get books.

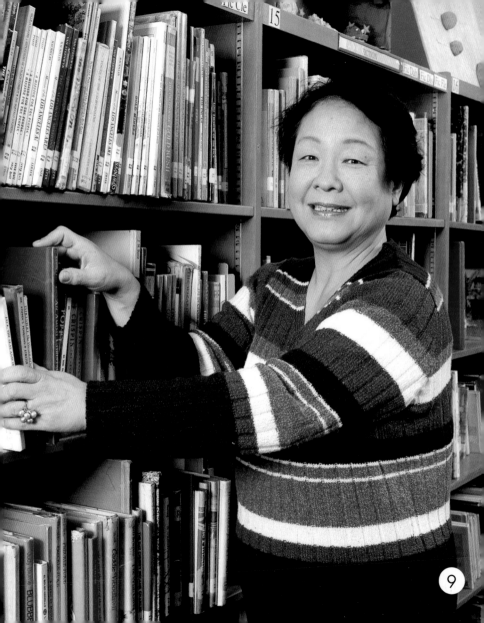

You can get stamps.

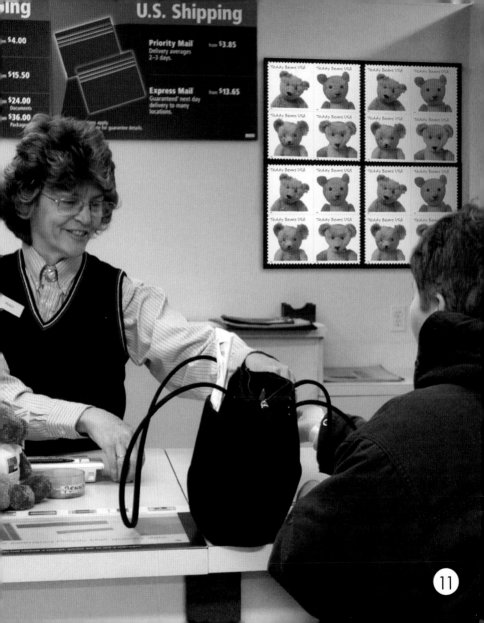

You can get shoes.

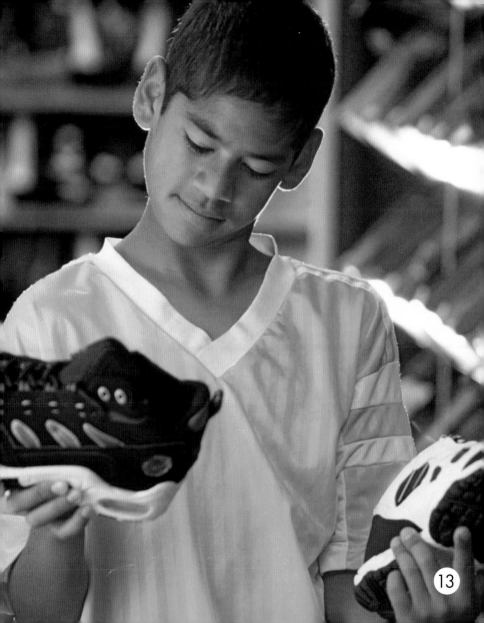

You can get haircuts.

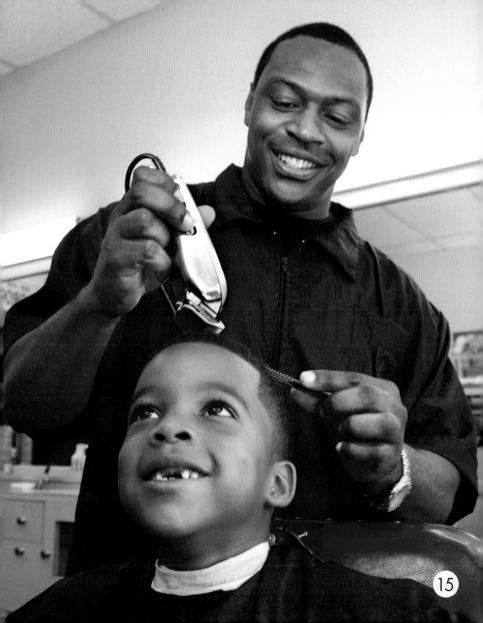

You can get pizza!

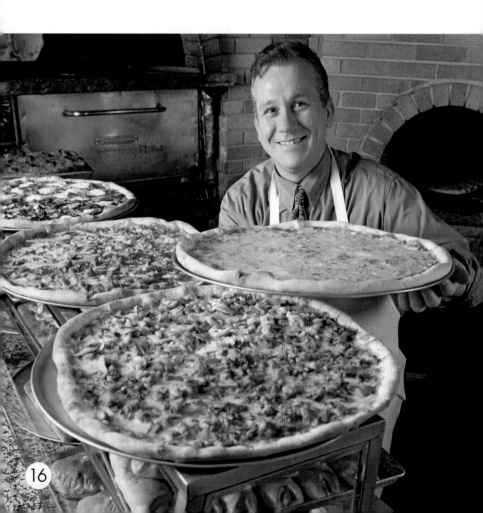